T0114845

A TABLE OF
VISIONS

TO REVIVE
THE NATION

W. J. WEBB

authorHOUSE®

AuthorHouse™
1663 Liberty Drive
Bloomington, IN 47403
www.authorhouse.com
Phone: 833-262-8899

Published by AuthorHouse 02/24/2021

ISBN: 978-1-6655-0319-8 (sc)
ISBN: 978-1-6655-0318-1 (e)

Library of Congress Control Number: 2020919452

Print information available on the last page.

Any people depicted in stock imagery provided by Getty Images are models, and such images are being used for illustrative purposes only. Certain stock imagery © Getty Images.

This book is printed on acid-free paper.

Scriptures are taken from the King James Version of the Bible.

Contents

Preface

A Table of Visions is written for four primary reasons. First, it is to affirm that America is an exceptionally blessed Nation by God. Secondly, an enumeration of the foundations of the blessings. Thirdly, how the people of the Nation must maintain the blessings. Lastly, the dire necessity of sharing the blessings in order to maintain the blessings. It is most unfortunate, and even tragic, that most Americans are not aware of the exceptional blessings that have been bestowed upon the American Nation. This lack of vital knowledge about the exceptional blessings of America is a failure of America's educational, religious, social and political systems. It is very obvious that most inhabitants of America are oblivious to the special grace that God has shed upon America. God's blessings have been taken for granted. Tragically, too many inhabitants of America are in such intense denial about God and God's special blessings to America, that it would take the loss of the blessings to awake them to the realization of the blessed America.

A Table of Visions is written to awake Americans of these blessings before it is too late. It is written to change the 21st Century trajectory of America that denies and mocks the blessings of God and thereby precipitating the decline and destruction of America. Such a catastrophic disaster would be unparalleled in human history. America has reached a tipping point in this 21st Century where it can no longer ignore the divine blessings that have undergirded the blessings, prosperity and individual liberties of the American people.

The blessings that gave rise to America as a world power in the 19th and 20th centuries were not accidental or happenstance. This book is written to enlighten Americans and the world about the biblical values of God that made America a blessed nation of the earth. It is written to alert God fearing Americans to quickly engage in the challenge of reconnecting and mending those survival values that blessed America. It was President Eisenhower who alluded to these values by his most memorable statement, "America is great because she is good. If she ceases to be good, she will cease to be great." Without those values and the blessings alluded to by President Eisenhower, not only will America cease to be great, the more realistic prospect of America is that it will, "cease to exist."

The foundation values of America were based on the Judea-Christian values contained in the Holy Bible; The Declaration of Independence, United States Constitution, The Pledge of Allegiance of One Nation Under God, and the American Motto, "In God We Trust." and a democratic form of government by the people, for the people and of the people. The adoption of these documents and values created a culture with the ideals of liberty, justice, individual freedom, free enterprise systems, due process of law and required public education. These values were preached and taught in the churches, homes and schools. The American institutions and the culture at large were permeated and saturated with these founding ethical and moral values that empowered the spirit of the Nation with hope, dreams, visions and unlimited possibilities.

The biblical values along with the values engendered by the founding and foundational creeds of America had the effect of unleashing unparalleled individual creativity and innovations in all areas of life. This fertile, libertarian enrichment gave rise to the automobile and the airplane among thousands of other inventions. This young nation survived a civil war in 1863. It produced outstanding world champions, such as Joe Louis and Jesse Owens. It produced some of the greatest musicians that the world has ever known in Mahalia Jackson and Paul Robeson. This young nation explored outer space and landed a man on the moon. This young American Nation, along with other allied nations defeated the Nazis in World War II. America is the primary guardian of the individual freedom that nations of the world enjoy. These values have put America in a position to be able to militarily deter nations that do not value individual freedom. The peace, freedom, prosperity and military might of America depend upon the biblical, ethical and moral values that have been described. God's foundational and unfolding blessings of America rest upon these values.

It is critical for the continued peace, prosperity and existence of America to continue to embrace, practice and share these blessings and God inspired values with all Americans and the world. These values can be taught. These values can be transmitted. A Table of Visions consist of the core survival values and blessings from God. These core values have been abbreviated and highlighted for rapid dissemination throughout America and the world to maintain and expand the individual freedom and life giving blessings to America and world.

It is critical that America recognizes that God blessed America in an exceptional way because America was founded upon biblical doctrines that acknowledge God, the truth of the Bible and the Savior, Jesus Christ. God's blessings are not limited to America. America has the responsibility and duty to share these blessings with the world. God loves the whole world and wants all people to be blessed. A Table of Visions is an effort to share God's biblical knowledge, truth, wisdom, understanding and love with all Americans and all the world. GOD DECLARES THAT HIS WORD WILL NOT RETURN UNTO HIM VOID. (Isaiah 55:11)

"So shall my word be that goeth forth out of my mouth: it shall not return unto me void, but it shall accomplish that which I please, and it shall prosper in the thing whereto I sent it."

W.J.Webb

Chapter 1

Introduction
American Democracy and Public Theology

American Democracy and Public Theology
By
Willie James Webb

The 1 Amendment of the U.S. Constitution prohibits a theocratic form of government in the name of a religion. America has a democratic form of government that was created by a philosophy of Judea-Christian doctrines. The American Democracy proposes to be a representative form of government for the people, by the people and of the people. It is the longest lasting constitution of any other known government.

It is significant to note that Christian believers developed the American democratic form of government and constitution on September 17, 1787 at a time when there was no significant heterogeneity in America besides the native Americans and the Negro slaves. It is significant that these Christian believers developed a universal constitutional form of government that was inclusive of all people. However, the practice of this democracy excluded Black African American Slaves at this time in American history. Religions do not have a monopoly on the universal moral and ethical principles essential for the equitable administration, allocation, distribution and accountability for the goods, resources and services existing in the society. Therefore, the laws of the U. S. Constitution were not "religious" laws, but they were laws in congruence with truth, justice and righteousness.

God created and God requires specific laws and commandments to govern the conduct of all people regardless of their form of government or type of religion. God requires all leaders and all people to live according to the truth, justice, righteousness, goodness, mercy, love and the will of God. God's laws and principles are not arbitrary and do not depend on individual opinions for their validity. God's laws and principles are true, just, and righteous and based in reality. God's laws are not relative, neutral or fictional. They are real with real consequences. No person, nation or religion is exempt from God's laws and judgement.

God is the creator of the universe with absolute jurisdiction over everything and every being (Genesis). The earth and everything therein belongs to God (Psalm 24). God demands that every soul be subject to God (Romans 13:1). Contrary to the expressions of many judges and legal scholars, religion is not synonymous with God, the Bible or Jesus Christ. Religions are created and born in history. They also die. in history. However, God, the Bible and Jesus Christ are above history and human culture. The autonomous nature of man made by God, has free will to choose. Man can choose to ignore God, Jesus and the Bible. However, man's independent negative choice does not negate God, Jesus or the Bible. Man's independent choice does not excuse man's duty to obey God and God's commandments. Man's autonomous free will does not excuse man's rebellious spirit against God. God's jurisdiction is inescapable. His commandments cannot be suspended. Personal responsibility and accountability to God cannot be delegated or evaded. God's divine laws and natural laws are absolutely supreme. MANMADE LAWS ARE ONLY VALID WHEN THEY ARE CONGRUENT WITH GOD'S LAWS & WILL.

JUSTICE REQUIRES SYSTEMS OF MERIT
Government Systems without Merit
Perpetuate Corruption & Injustice

In a democratic form of government the allocation of human resources, goods and services of the government require systems, laws, regulations, policies and procedures of equitable merit. This is to assure that each person receives his or her dues according to fairness and justice. Arbitrary systems of non-merit favoritism create confusion, corruption and chaos.

The United States Government as well as state governments have histories of personnel administration merit systems. Policies and procedures were in place that required the documentation of the respective qualifications as well as the administration of written and oral examinations to be objective in the selection of applicants based on merit. It was common practice in the 1950s, 1960s and 1970s to go through a merit- based qualification process for government jobs and contracts. During this period of time, the State of Georgia had a merit system that processed applicants for jobs. The State of Georgia also had an office called GOFEP (Georgia Office of Fair Employment Practice). These merit- based systems have been discontinued. What are the motives and rationale for this discontinuation of merit systems?

The advent of the 1964 Civil Rights Act and the creation of the EEOC (Equal Employment Opportunity Commission) engendered some hope for equitable merit- based fairness and justice in government employment and in the allocation of other government resources and services. Affirmative action programs were also created to bridge the gaps of those who were behind due to pass racial and other forms of discrimination. However, the intended purpose of the 1964 Civil Rights Act and the EEOC have not accomplished the intended goals and objectives. The corruption and dysfunctionality in EEOC and the judicial system have diluted and nullified equitable fairness, systems of merit and judicial justice. The unethical and immoral forces of secularism appear to be pushing the ideas, concepts and the notions of merit systems out of the culture. Have thoughtful people considered a society without justice?

Merit systems in government are being replaced with arbitrary, partisan political identity, ethnocentric favoritism systems. Government personnel systems are becoming openly weaponized with arrogant administrative intimidation, re-constitutional procedures, dictatorial dismissals, punitive, vindictive no hire lists or no rehire black lists; without any DUE PROCESS OF LAW as required by the U. S. Constitution. There are serious consequences when human justice is violated. Human justice requires merit systems in the allocation of God's resources and values. Justice requires government merit systems. Injustice is a threat to democracy. Social injustice violates human rights. Injustice is a threat to America. Injustice is a threat to civilization. THE RESTORATION OF MERIT SYSTEMS AND JUSTICE IN THE AMERICA GOVERNMENT MUST BE A TOP PRIORITY FOR SURVIVAL AS A NATION!

THE FIGHT FOR LIFE

"Put on the whole armour of God, that ye may be able to
stand against the wiles of the devil." (Ephesians 6:11}

The perplexities and complexities of societal cultural diversity and human heterogeneous problems require public theologians with the expertise of SOCIAL CHEMISTS, POLITICAL PHYSICISTS, LEGAL MATHEMATICIANS and THEOLOGICAL ETHICISTS. One dimensional simplistic proposals and solutions are not adequate to address the multidimensional complex problems humanity faces in this 21st Century.

An understanding of SOCIAL CHEMISTRY is necessary to understand the social dynamics of the effects of the social and psychological interactions of the various ethnic and diverse groups of people in America along with their various ideologies and idiosyncrasies. How can these integrated, associated mixtures be facilitated for good?

An understanding of POLITICAL PHYSICS is essential to understand the influences of political decisions, their social impact, allocation and use of resources, social change, gentrification, community development, community health and quality of life. How competent and ethical are the driving political forces?

An understanding of LEGAL MATHEMATICS is essential in sorting, selecting and computing the applicable, overlapping, intertwined myriad statutory, natural and divine laws in the effort to render true justice and equity to all persons.

An understanding of RELIGIOUS ETHICS is essential for determining in the midst of the human complexities; that which is true, equitable, just, good, merciful and loving as authorized by the Will and Witness of GOD for the common good.

"Study to show thyself approved unto God, a workman that needeth not to be ashamed, rightly dividing the word of truth." (2Timothy 2:15)

WHAT ARE THE CONSEQUENCES OF A SILENT CHURCH?
Humanity's Vital Need for the Word of God
(The Christian Institute of Public Theology)

A silent Church fails to plant and cultivate seeds of life. This moral failure and ethical duty allow evil seeds of destruction and death to grow and multiply. The teaching, preaching and practicing the Biblical Word of God are so vital that human life is aborted, withers, deteriorates, and destructs without God's Word. God's Word enlightens the mind, nurtures the body and soul. God's Biblical Word gives life, shares life and protects life. Jesus declares that he came to give life and to give it "more abundantly." John 3:16 proclaims that God so loved the world, "that He gave his only begotten Son, that whosoever believe in him should not perish, but have eternal life."

The destructive consequences of the deprivation of the Biblical Word of God, can be measured, predicted and correlated with the following human, cultural and societal degeneration and deterioration:

___1. Religious Idolatry. (The worship of idol and false gods.)

___2. Mental Confusion. (Mental disorders and insanity.)

___3. Human Disorders. (Hatred, personality dysfunctions and social maladjustments.)

___4. Spiritual Wickedness. (Orientation and practice of evil behavior against life.)

___5. Cultural Dysfunction. (Confusion of social roles, values and traditions.)

___6. Government Corruption. (Abuse, misuse & weaponization of government authority.)

___7. Political Destabilization. (Divisive political identity, ethnic & ideological confusion.)

___8. Social upheavals, crime. (Disrespect for law, order, human life & civilization.)

___9. Institutional Dysfunctions. (Dysfunctional families, education, religious, business, etc.)

___10. Social/economic/political/religious/cultural/chaos. (Devoid of humane survival values)

___11. Chaotic, confused, disordered, corrupted government and culture. (Decline of civility.)

___12. National catastrophic disruption of civilized living, humane living and quality of life. (Total human ruin; loss of freedom, humanity, civility, government, lives, nationhood)

These twelve destructive consequences of the silent Church are not mysterious. They have been predicated on the predictability of human nature through numerous demonstrations that have been played out on the real stage of history for thousands of years. No nation in history has survived the worship and the practice of secularism, materialism, atheism and the willful rebellion against the Word of God. The words of Hosea (Hosea 4:6) still rings true, "My people are destroyed for lack of knowledge... forgotten the law of God." This knowledge refers to theological knowledge (knowledge about God.). The loving God has given mankind a true historical time tested rule book and blueprint for living. This Rule Book and Blueprint for living is known as THE HOLY BIBLE. THE TIME IS HERE WHEN CHURCH LEADERS AND BELIEVERS MUST SEND FORTH GOD'S WORD THROUGH EVERY MEDIA POSSIBLE WITH URGENCY THROUGHOUT THE EARTH. GOD'S WORD WILL NOT RETURN VOID (Isaiah 55:11).

The Christian's Sacred Duty

God's Spiritual Guidance and Blessings for Mankind

___1. Fear God, and keep his commandments: for this is the whole duty of man. (Eccles. 2:13)

___2. Let this mind be in you which was also in Christ Jesus. (Philippians 2:5)

___3. Thou shall love the Lord thy God with all thy heart, and with all soul, and with all thy Mind. (Matthew 22:37)

___4. Thou shall love thy neighbor as thyself. (Matthew 22:39)

___5. Be fruitful, and multiply, and replenish the earth, and subdue It: and have dominion over the fish of the sea, and over the fowl of the air, and over every living thing that moves upon the earth. (Genesis 1:28)

___6. But seek ye first the kingdom of God, and his righteousness; and all these things shall be added unto you. (Matthew 6:33)

___7. Except a man be born again, he cannot see the kingdom of God. (John 3:3). Marvel not That I said unto thee, you must be born again. (John 3:7)

___8. But be ye transformed by the renewing of your mind, that ye may prove what is that Good, and acceptable, and perfect, will of God. (Romans 12:2)

___9. Fight the good fight of faith, lay hold on eternal life. (1Timothy)

___10. Be strong in the grace that is in Christ Jesus. (2Timothy 2:1)

___11. Preach the word; be instant in season, out of season; reprove, rebuke, exhort with all long suffering and doctrine. (2Timothy 4:2)

___12. But watch thou in all things, endure afflictions, do the work of an evangelist, make full Proof of thy ministry. (2Timothy 4:5)

___13. I have fought a good fight, I have finished my course, I have kept the faith. (2Tim. 4-7)

___14. Son of man, I have made thee a watchman unto the house of Israel: Therefore, hear the word at my mouth, and give them warning from me. (Ezekiel 3:17)

___15. Warn the wicked. (Ezekiel 3:18-19). Warn the righteous. (Ezekiel 3:20-21)

___16. Therefore, let us not sleep, as do others, but let us watch and be sober. (Thessalonians 5:6)

___17. Rejoice evermore. Pray without ceasing. In everything give thanks. (Thessalonians 5:16-18)

___18. I press toward the mark for the prize of the high calling of God in Christ Jesus. (Philippians 3:14)

___19. 19. But let judgment run down as waters, and righteousness as a mighty stream. (Amos 5:24)

___20. Draw nigh unto God, and he will draw nigh unto you. (James 4:8)

Chapter 2

The Biblical Blessed Word

GOD'S BLESSINGS
And
COMMANDMENTS
To The
MAN AND WOMAN

So God created man in his own image, in the Image of God created he him; male and female created he them. And God blessed them, and God said unto them, Be fruitful and multiply, and replenish the earth, and subdue it: and have dominion over the fish of the sea, and over the fowl of the air, and over every living thing that moveth upon the earth.

(Genesis 1:27-28)

THE HOLY BIBLE

GOD'S

UNIVERSAL
STANDARDS
FOR
ALL PEOPLE &
ALL NATIONS

T

H

E

BIBLE

IS

THE VITAL BOOK

OF

KNOWLEDGE AND WISDOM

LOVE AND TRUTH

ABUNDANT AND ETERNAL

LIFE

THE
HOLY BIBLE

GOD'S
COMMANDMENTS
AND JUDGMENTS
FOR
ALL PEOPLE
ALL NATIONS
ALL TIME

THE
BIBLE

GOD'S GUIDANCE

FOR
NATIONS
AND
HUMANITY

BIBLICAL TRUTH AND KNOWLEDGE @ CHRIST

PREVENT

SELF-RIGHTEOUSNESS AND JUDGMENT OF OTHERS

The BIBLE IS
The AUTHORIZED
VALIDATION
Of
TRUTH and LOVE
LAW and JUSTICE

THE BIBLE IS NOT JUST A MESSAGE FOR THE CHURCH & BELIEVERS.

IT HAS A MESSAGE FOR THE NATIONS, THEIR HEADS AND LEADERS.

THE MESSAGE OF THE BIBLE IS URGENT AND VITAL FOR ALL PEOPLE!

"IN GOD WE TRUST"

IS INVALIDATED

WHEN
GOD'S BIBLICAL
WORD
IS
DENIGRATED
&ALIENATED

THE BIBLE
IS
AN
IN-EXHAUSTIBLE
SOURCE
OF
KNOWLEDGE
& WISDOM
FOR
LIFE & LIVING

RECOGNITION REVERENCE GRATITUDE for the Wonderful Counsellor Mighty God Everlasting Father Prince of Peace

For unto us a child is born, unto us a son is given: and the government shall be upon his shoulder: and his name shall be called Wonderful, Counsellor, The mighty God, The everlasting Father, The Prince of Peace. Of the increase of his government and peace there shall be no end, upon the throne of David, and upon his Kingdom, to order it, and to establish it with judgment and justice from henceforth and even forever.

(Isaiah 9:6-7)

THE BIBLE IS THE MOST WIDELY KNOWN BOOK OF HISTORY.

JESUS CHRIST IS THE MOST CELEBRATED AND EXALTED PERSON OF ALL HISTORY.

HAVE YOU STUDIED THE BIBLE?   DO YOU KNOW JESUS?

NO MAN AND NO

MANMADE INSTITUTIONS

HAVE AUTHORITY

OVER THE CANONIZED

HOLY BIBLE

THE
BIBLE GAVE BIRTH TO:

Declaration of Independence
United States Constitution
Pledge of Allegiance to US Flag
In God We Trust on Currency
One Nation under God Motto
Religious Freedom & Churches
Required Education for Youth
The Free Enterprise System
AMERICAN DEMOCRACY

Ye are a chosen generation, a royal priesthood, an holy nation,
a peculiar people; that you should show forth the praises
of him who has called you out of darkness (I Ptr 2:9).

Chapter 3

Hierarchy of Authority

HIERARCHY
OF
AUTHORITY

Nation Under God
In God We Trust
Holy Bible
U.S. Constitution
Declaration of
Independence

For Justice-Righteousness-Liberty-Equality-Mercy

BLESSED
IS THE NATION THAT EMBRACES THE BIBLE ITS ENDURING TRUTHS, SOUND DOCTRINES, KNOWLEDGE, WISDOM AND ENLIGHTENMENT ABOUT LIFE & LIVING; THE WAYS, WISDOM, LOVE AND WILL OF GOD IN JESUS CHRIST.

"IN GOD WE TRUST"

IS INVALIDATED

WHEN
GOD'S BIBLICAL WORD
IS
DENIGRATED
& ALIENATED

IT IS CRITICAL FOR
NATIONS UNDER
GOD IN THE AGE OF
TECHNOLOGY-

TO

BIBLICALLY   EDUCATE
ITS PEOPLE ABOUT GOD
AND VICTORIOUS LIVING
IN JESUS CHRIST

A NATION UNDER GOD WITH TRUST IN GOD

MUST PRIORITIZE BIBLICAL KNOWLEDGE ABOUT GOD

IN HOMES, CHURCHES, SCHOOLS, BUSINESS, INDUSTRY & GOVERNMENT!

"A NATION UNDER GOD",

IT IS A CONTRADICTION TO CLAIM TO BE A NATION UNDER GOD, AND OUTLAW THE BIBLE IN THE PUBLIC SCHOOLS AND IN THE PUBLIC SQUARE.

THE BIBLE IS THE GREATEST SOURCE OF KNOWLEDGE ABOUT GOD. WE MUST GET REAL AND LIVE UP TO THE NOBLE CLAIM, "A NATION UNDER GOD."

LAWYERS & JUDGES
WITHOUT
BIBLICAL KNOWLEDGE

DISPARAGE JUSTICE
IGNORE TRUTH
DISREGARD
RIGHTEOUSNESS
AND
INSULT GOD

A NATION UNDER GOD

MUST EMBRACE THE BIBLE

THE WORD OF GOD

In the beginning was the Word, and the Word was with God, and the Word was God (Jn 1:1).

And the Word was made flesh, and dwelt among us. (Jn 1:14).

IT IS CRITICAL FOR
NATIONS UNDER GOD IN
THEAGEOFTECHNOLOGY

TO

BIBLICALLY EDUCATE
ITS PEOPLE ABOUT GOD
AND VICTORIOUS LIVING
IN JESUS CHRIST

U. S. CONSTITUTION
Amendment No 5
Due Process of Law and Compensation

"No person shall be.....
deprived of life, liberty,
or property, without due
process of law; nor Shall
private property be taken
for public use, without
just compensation."

THE DENIAL
Of
DUE PROCESS
OF LAW

VIOLATES
HUMAN RIGHTS

And The
U. S. Constitution

POLITICALLY SPEAKING DOES YOUR CANDIDATE REPRESENT:
-BIBLE VALUES?
-YOUR FAITH?
-YOUR COMMUNITY?
-YOUR PEOPLE?
YOUR COUNTRY?
-JESUS CHRIST?
-CREATOR GOD?

THE UNIVERSAL GREAT COMMANDMENT

Jesus said unto him, Thou shall love the Lord thy God with all thy heart, and with all thy soul, and with all thy mind.

This is the first and great commandment.

And the second is like unto it, Thou shall love thy neighbor as thy self.

On these two commandments hang all the law and the prophets.

(Matthew 22:37-40)

WEAPONIZATION OF GOVERNMENT AGAINST THE PEOPLE MUST BE RESISTED AND ELIMINATED

Chapter 4

Battle Against Injustice

A CIVILIZED GOVERNMENT PROTECTS INALIENABLE HUMAN RIGHTS
SOCIAL JUSTICE IS THE DUTY OF A DEMOCRATIC GOVERNMENT

The government protection of the inalienable God given human rights fosters the optimum actualization of the God given human potential to achieve and experience the following blessings of God to:

_____1. Embrace the reality of truth.
_____2. Seek the life giving and enlightenment of knowledge.
_____3. Experience the balance and congruence of justice.
_____4. Appreciate and extol the virtues of goodness.
_____5. Follow the ways of righteousness.
_____6. Embrace and savor the preciousness and value of love.
_____7. Enjoy and behold the esthetic beauty of artistic expressions.
_____8. See and visualize the illumination of light and enlightenment.
_____9. Wait with patience for the resilience of hope.
_____10. Hold on and hold out with the perseverance of faith.
_____11. Realize the gift and understanding of wisdom.
_____12. Use wisely and gratefully the autonomy of freedom.

THE LOVING GOD OF LOVE HAS ENDOWED MANKIND WITH UNLIMITED AND INEXHAUSTIBLE POTENTIALS FOR THE GOOD LIFE, THE ABUNDANT LIFE AND EVEN ETERNAL LIFE. IT IS WRITTEN AND CONFIRMED IN THE BIBLICAL WORD OF GOD! Governments are instituted to protect these inalienable rights from God!

The U.S. Constitution Bill of Rights

The Bill of Rights of the U.S. Constitution must be revisited to safeguard and protect the threatened fragile human and Civil Rights of the Black Americans, the off springs of slaves in America during this critical time of massive immigration, moral decay and gentrification.

The following two Amendments of the Bill of Rights offer the best legal foundation to protect and safeguard the fragile "unalienable rights," of Black Americans. They are the 5th Amendment and the 14th Amendment:

Amendment 5

No person shall be held to answer for a capital, or otherwise infamous crime, unless on a presentment or indictment of a grand jury, except in cases arising in the land or naval forces, or in the militia, when in actual service in time of war or public danger; nor shall any person be subject for the same offense to be twice put in jeopardy of life or limb; nor shall be compelled in any criminal case to be a witness against himself, nor be deprived of life, liberty, or property, without due process of law; nor shall private property be taken for public use, without just compensation.

NOTE: "without due process of law," and, "without just compensation," have broad bases for interpretation. Legal cases can be made with this Amendment to safeguard and protect the property rights of Black Americans in Atlanta and other places in America.

Amendment 14

All persons born or naturalized in the United States and subject to the jurisdiction thereof, are citizens of the United States and of the state wherein they reside. No state shall make or enforce any law which shall abridge the privileges or immunities of citizens of the United States; nor shall any state deprive any person of life, liberty, or property, without due process of law; nor deny to any person within its jurisdiction the equal protection of the laws.

NOTE: Amendment 14 is the premier amendment that provided a legal foundation for the landmark 1964 Civil Rights Act. This Amendment 14 and the 1964 Civil Rights Act can be revisited, especially for the property right aspect. THE DUE PROCESS OF LAW guaranteed by the United States Constitution is being violated by perpetrators and judicial systems every day in the week. U.S. CITIZENS MUST DEMAND THAT THE LAW BE RESPECTED & OBSERVED.

WARFARE AGAINST WICKEDNESS

For we wrestle not against flesh and blood, but against principalities, against powers, against the rulers of the darkness of this world, against spiritual wickedness in high places.

(Ephesians 6:12)

This know also, that in the last days perilous times shall come. For men shall be lovers of their own selves, covetous, boasters, proud, blasphemers, disobedient to parents, unthankful, unholy.

Without natural affection, trucebreakers, false accusers, incontinent, fierce, despisers of those that are good, Traitors, heady, high-minded, lovers of pleasures more than lovers of God; Having a form of godliness, but denying the power thereof: from such turn away.

(2Timothy 3:1-5)

For the time will come when they will not endure sound doctrine; but after their own lusts shall ...turn away their ears from the truth. (2Timothy 4:3-4)

INJUSTICE DIMINISHES

The HUMAN POTENTIAL

INJUSTICE IS A WICKED ACT OF VIOLENCE

Seek good and not evil that you may live: and so the Lord, the God of hosts, shall be with you, as you have spoken. Hate the evil, and love the good, and establish judgment in the gate: it may be that the Lord God of hosts will be gracious unto the remnant of Joseph. (Amos 5:14-15)

I hate, I despise your feast days, and I will not smell in your solemn assemblies. Though you offer me burnt offerings and your meat offerings. I will not accept them: neither will I regard the peace offerings of your fat beasts. Take thou away from me the noise of thy songs; for I will not hear the melody of thy viols. But let judgment run down as waters, and righteousness as a mighty stream. (Amos 5:21-24)

Behold, the days come, saith the Lord God, that I will send a famine in the land, not a famine of bread, nor a thirst for water, but of hearing the words of the Lord. (Amos 8:11)

THE UNITED STATES OF AMERICA UNITED RESOLVE
UNITED STATES AND UNITED PEOPLE

The National Decision and Resolve to Live up to the Founding American Creeds:

___1. ONE NATION UNDER GOD.

___2. IN GOD WE TRUST.

___3. THE SELF EVIDENTIARY TRUTHS THAT ALL MEN ARE CREATED EQUAL.

___4. ALL MEN (WOMEN INCLUSIVE) ARE ENDOWED BY THEIR CREATOR WITH CERTAIN INALIENABLE RIGHTS;

___5. AMONG THESE RIGHTS; ARE LIFE, LIBERTY AND THE PURSUIT OF HAPPINESS;

___6. WITH CITIZENSHIP RIGHTS OF THE DUE PROCESS OF LAW; AS A PREREQUISITE TO THE DEPRIVATION OF LIFE, LIBERTY AND PROPERTY;

___7. AND THE RIGHT TO THE EQUAL PROTECTION OF THE LAW.

THE FOUNDATIONAL MANDATED AMERICAN CREEDS ARE UNMISTAKABLY CLEAR; AS A NATION SUBSCRIBING TO EVIDENTIARY TRUTHS; GOD GIVEN HUMAN RIGHTS, WITH EQUAL PROTECTION OF THE LAW; AND AS A NATION UNDER GOD.

THE UNITED STATES OF THE AMERICAN GOVERNMENT AND NATION OF PEOPLE MUST DISAVOW ATHEISTIC AND SATANIC SPIRITS, THAT WAGE WARS OF WICKEDNESS AGAINST THE SACRED VALUES, HE HOLY BIBLE, THE UNITED STATES' CONSTITUTION, THE SOUND DOCTRINES, THE SOCIAL JUSTICE, THE LIGHT OF TRUTH, AND THE REVERENCE OF GOD, OF THE UNITED STATES OF AMERICA, AND THE PEOPLE OF GOD.

BE NOT DECEIVED. GOD IS NOT MOCKED. YOU REAP WHAT YOU SOW.

(Galatians 6:7)

U.S. CONSTITUTION
Amendment No 5
Due Process of Law and Compensation

''No person shall be..... Deprived of life, liberty, or property, without due process of law; nor shall private property be taken for public use, without just compensation.''

DESTROYING PAST HISTORICAL SYMBOLS

IGNORES PRESENT PERVASIVE EVIL

The Christian Institute of Public Theolog

THE NEW COMMANDMENT

A new commandment I give unto you, that you love one another; as I have loved you, that you also love one another.

(John 13:34)

By this shall all men know that you are my disciples, if you have love one to another.

(John 13:35)

MENTAL, SPIRITUAL & ADDICTIVE DISORDERS

There is a way which seem right unto a man, but the end thereof are the ways of death. (Proverbs 14:12)

The way of a fool is right in his own eyes: but he that hearkens to counsel is wise. (Proverbs 12:15)

In those days there was no king in Israel: every man did that which was right in his own eyes. (Judges 21:25)

Woe unto them that call evil good, and good evil; that put darkness for light, and light for darkness; that put bitter for sweet, and sweet for bitter! Woe unto them that are wise in their own eyes, and prudent in their own sight! Woe unto them that are mighty to drink wine, and men of strength to mingle strong drink: which justify the wicked for reward, and take away the righteousness of the righteous from him! (Isaiah 5:20-23)

DESTRUCTION OF DORMANT MONUMENTS

IS INFANTILE SUPERFLUOUS FUTILITY

The Christian Institute of Public Theology

HUMANS HAVE A DUTY

TO

CREATE

BEAUTY

The Christian Institute of Public Theology

PROACTIVE LOVE

-PREVENTS-

REACTIVE HATRED

The Christian Institute of Public Theology

THE DESIRE FOR HUMAN VALIDATION

Instead of

GOD'S DECLARATION

Becomes a
DEHUMANIZING ABOMINATION

The Christian Institute of Public Theology

G OD'S CREATION

IS

COSMOS

NOT

CHAOS

PUT ON

THE WHOLE ARMOR OF GOD

TO PRACTICE

THE WHOLE GOSPEL

OF

PUBLIC THEOLOGY

The Christian Institute of Public Theology

THE ETHICAL TEST FOR TRUTH

Is the belief, position, behavior Biblically authorized by God?

Does the belief, position or behavior enhance the quality and totality of human life?

Does the belief, position or behavior acknowledge and glorify God?

The Christian Institute of Public Theology

POLITICALLY SPEAKING DOES YOUR CANDIDATE REPRESENT:

-BIBLE VALUES?

-YOUR FAITH?

-YOUR COMMUNITY?

-YOUR PEOPLE?

-YOUR COUNTRY?

-JESUS CHRIST?

-CREATOR GOD?

RESIST-RESIST

SOCIALISTIC

SECULARISTIC

MILITARISTIC
ATHEISTIC

PEOPLE CONTROL

POLITICAL
IDEOLOGIES.

The Public Theologian

Chapter 5

The Blessings of Education

PROACTIVE EDUCATION

-PREVENTS-

RESULTING DEPRIVATION

EDUCATE MINDS WITH TRUTH

TRANSFORM HEARTS WITH LOVE

ENHANCE LIFE WITH KNOWLEDGE

Take fast hold of instruction; let her not go: keep her; for she is thy life. (Proverbs 4:13); The fear of the Lord is the beginning of wisdom: and knowledge of the holy is understanding. (Proverbs 9:10)

CHRISTIAN CHURCHES GAVE BIRTH TO:

Public Schools and Required Education for Children as well as the Institutions of Higher Education.

Take fast hold of instruction; Let her not go: Keep her; for she is thy life. (Proverbs 4:13)

Train up a child in the way he should go: and when he is old, he will not depart from it. (Proverbs 22:6)

GEORGIALAW HOUSEBILL605

Improved Student Learning Environment and Discipline Act. Signed and Dated by Governor Barnes: 4/23/1999

Local District Action Needed:

___1. Local Boards must implement a Comprehensive Character Education Program for levels K-12 by the Beginning of the 2000-2001School Year.

___2. This Program must focus on the student's Development of the following Character Traits: (1) Courage, (2) Patriotism, (3) Citizenship, (4) Honesty, (5) Fairness, (6) Respect for Others, (7) Kindness, (8) Cooperation, (9) Self Respect, (10) Courtesy, (11) Compassion, (12) Tolerance, (13) Diligence, (14) Generosity,(15) Punctuality,(16) Creativity, (17) Sportsmanship, (18) Loyalty,(19) Perseverance, (20) Cleanliness, (21) Cheerfulness, (22) School Pride, (23) Respect for Environment, (24) Respect for the Creator, (25) Self-Control, (26) Patience, (27) Virtue.

Fundamental Traits for Teaching Character Education
(Georgia Law 20-2-145- House Bill605, 1999)

___1. Cheerfulness   .How to be positive, pleasant & Encouraging.

___2. Citizenship   How to be a responsible member of society.

___3. Compassion   A caring considerate concern for life & others.

___4. Cleanliness   Personal & hygienic care taking of environment.

___5. Cooperation   Learn and practice teamwork with others.

___6. Courtesy   Extend friendliness & hospitality to others.

___7. Courage   Learn to be brave and take a stand for righteousness.

___8. Creativity   Use your God given gifts & intelligence to be creative.

___9. Diligence   Don't give up. Hold on. Endure. Fight the good fight.

___10. Fairness   Treat all persons with respect. Give all their dues.

___11. Generosity   Develop a spirit of giving and sharing goods & services.

___12. Honesty   Be real, bona-fide, sincere, true, ethical and authentic.

___13. Kindness   Be pleasant, affirming, helpful, positive, deligtful.

___14. Loyalty   Be reliable, dependable, committed, trustworthy.

___15. Patriotism   Love, respect, concern and loyalty to America, your nation.

___16. Patience   Learn to wait with hope and fond expectation for the future.

___17. Perseverance	A faith and resolve to work & struggle until victory is won.
___18. Punctuality	Observe considerations for more precise time schedule.
___19. Respect for Creator	Reverence and humility for God the Creator of the universe.
___20. Respect for others	Esteem the significance and sacredness of human life.
___21. Respect for Environment	Replenish, keep clean, safe, productive, healthy & livable.
___22. Self-Respect	Recognize yourself as a sacred being of integrity with human dignity and made in the image of God.
___23. Self-control	.Be guided by truth, knowledge, wisdom, understanding, Justice, righteousness and the Biblical Word of God.
___24. Sportsmanship	.Work honestly. Play Fairly. Loose gracefully. Endeavor to always do your best. Claim a successful identity in God.
___25. School Pride	.Help your school achieve academic excellence, cultural enrichment, responsible leadership, noble character development and humanitarian service to mankind.
___26. Temperance	How to keep your mind, emotions and behavior responsibly balanced in the world of pragmatic reality.
___27. Virtue	Embrace those values that represent the Excellency of the GOOD, TRUTH AND THE BEAUTIFUL.

TO ALL AMERICANS AND ALL EDUCATIONAL INSTITUTIONS

THE CULTURE CRISIS MANDATES EDUCATION FOR THE WHOLE PERSON: THE HEAD, HEART, HANDS & HEALTH
(HUMAN HATRED AND TECHNOLOGY HAVE MADE THIS AN URGENT NECESSITY)

CARE   EDUCATION

C haracter   **E** ducation
A rtistic   **E** ducation
R eligious   **E** ducation
E thical   **E** ducation

MUST   UNDERGIRD   AND   GUIDE

S T E M   EDUCATION

S cience   **E** ducation
T echnology   **E** ducation
E ngineering   **E** ducation
M ath   **E** ducation

"THE HUMAN NATURE OF MAN MUST BE NURTURED
BY THE SPIRITUAL NATURE OF GOD"

PROACTIVE EDUCATION

-PREVENTS-

EXPRESSED IGNORANCE

EDUCATION

-FIRST
LEARN TO READ

-NEXT
READ TO LEARN
-THEN-
KEEP READING
& LEARNING

MIND
ENLIGHTENMENT

DISSPELLS
DARKNESS &
IGNORANCE

TEACH RESPECT

-AVOID-

ARROGANCE & VAINGLORY

TRUE ART IS AN AUTHENTIC ELEVATED EXPRESSED THOUGHT

Unsound Doctrines

Corrupt & Poison the

Culture

BIBLICAL KNOWLEDGE AND ETHICAL VALUES

MUST BE PREREQUISITES FOR ALL TEACHERS ESPECIALLY FOR CHILDREN & YOUTH

FAILING PUBLIC SCHOOLS

MUST BE OUTLAWED NOW

ALL PUBLIC SCHOOLS

MUST BE

SUCCESS SCHOOLS

CIVIL
POSITIVITY

INCREASES

HUMAN
POSSIBILITY

Technology Without Theology Is Irresponsible and Dangerous

TEACH RESPECT

-AVOID-

ARROGANCE & VAINGLORY

THE TESTS FOR SPIRITUAL DISCERNMENT

Beloved, believe not every spirit, but try the spirits whether they are of God: because many false prophets Are gone out into the world. Hereby know you the spirit of God: Every spirit that confesses that Jesus Christ is come in the flesh is of God.

(John 4:1-2)

And every spirit that confesses not that Jesus Christ is come in the flesh is not of God: and this is that spirit of antichrist, whereof you have heard that it should come; And even now already is it in the world.

(1John 4:3)

For many deceivers are entered into the world, who confess not that Christ is come in the flesh. This is a deceiver and an antichrist.

(2John 1:7)

Unrighteousness
Hatred
Injustice
Arrogance

VIOLATE AND DAMAGE

The Human Enterprise

ANY PRINCIPLE
THAT CAN NOT BE
UNIVERSALIZED

IS NOT

A VALID PRINCIPLE
(Kant)

CHILDREN (also)

NEED MOTHERLY, PARENTAL,

ATTENTION, AFFECTION,

EMBRACING, ADORATION,

PLAYFUL GAMES, FUN THINGS,

EDUCATIONAL, SPIRITUAL &

HUMAN DEVELOPMENT

PUBLIC EDUCATION

CONGRUENT WITH TRUTH AND JUSTICE

ENHANCES RELIGIOUS LIBERTY & DEMOCRACY

Train up a child in the way he should go: and when he is old, he will not depart from it. (Proverbs 22:6}

My people are destroyed for lack of knowledge: because thou hast rejected knowledge, I will also reject thee, that thou shalt be no priest to me: seeing thou hast forgotten the law of thy God, I will also forget thy children. (Hosea 4:6)

Chapter 6

Humanity's Survival Values

THE CHOICE:

Religious Liberty

Or

Deathly Defiance

CONFORMITY TO THIS WORLD
DESTROYS SURVIVAL VALUES
The Need for Mind Renewal Transformation
(The Christian Institute of Public Theology)

___1. Where is the truth that has been lost in information and knowledge?

___2. Where is the wisdom that has been lost in understanding and reason?

___3. Where is the love that has been lost in affection and fellowship?

___4. Where is the compassion that has been lost in passion and relationships?

___5. Where is the humaneness that has been lost in humanity?

___6. Where is the civility that has been lost in civilization?

___7. Where is the wholeness that is lost in separation and division?

___8. Where is the beauty that has been lost in the essence of art?

___9. Where is the hope that has been lost in future expectations?

___10. Where is the love that is revealed and expressed in Jesus Christ?

___11. Where is the hope that has been lost in life's journey for the future?

___12. Where is the beauty that has been lost in the expression of the soul?

___13. Where is the joy that has been lost in the fellowship of living?

___14. Where is the belief that has been lost in life, abundant and eternal life?

___15. Where is the expectation that has been lost in the vindication of justice?

___16. Where is the faith that has been lost in the promises of God?

___17. Where is the courage that has been lost to live a victorious life?

___18. Where is the bravery that has been lost to confront the enemies of life?

___19. Where is the boldness that has been lost in standing for a righteous cause?

___20. Where are the minds that have lost the hunger for knowledge?

___21. Where are the souls that have lost the thirst and yearning for truth?

___22. Where are the north stars, the pillars of clouds, pillars of fire and the moral compass?

___23. Where is the psychology, anthropology, sociology and theology lost in technology?

___24. Where are the prophetic voices of truth, justice, freedom & love; lost in silence?

For to be carnally minded is death; but to be spiritually minded is life and peace. Because the carnal mind is enmity against God (Romans 8:7). So then they that are in the flesh cannot please God (Romans 8:8).

For who has known the mind of the Lord, that he may instruct him? But we have the mind of Christ (1Corinthians 2:16). Let this mind be in you which was also in Christ Jesus (Philippians 2:5). Thou wilt keep him in perfect peace, whose mind is stayed on thee (Isaiah 26:3).

There is neither Jew nor Greek, there is neither bond nor free, there is neither male nor female: for ye are all one in Christ Jesus(Galatians 3:28).

THE SPIRIT OF GOD AND BIBLICAL KNOWLEDGE ARE CRITICAL FOR HUMAN SURVIVAL VALUES

GOD'S RIGHTEOUSNESS
vs.
SELF-RIGHTEOUSNESS

Two men went up into the temple to pray; the one a pharisee, and the other a publican. The pharisee stood and prayed thus with himself, God, I thank thee, that I am not as other men are, extortioners, unjust, adulterers, or even as this publican. I fast twice in the week, I give tithes of all that I possess.

(Luke 18:10-12)

And the publican, standing afar off, would not lift up so much as his eyes unto heaven, but smote upon his breast, saying, God be merciful to me a sinner.

(Luke 18:13)

I tell you, that this man went down to his house justified rather than the other: for every one that exalts himself shall be abased, and he that humbles himself shall be exalted.

(Luke 18:14).

For they being ignorant of God's righteousness, and going about to establish their own righteousness, have not submitted themselves unto the righteousness of God.

(Romans 10:3)

THE TESTS FOR SPIRITUAL DISCERNMENT

Beloved, believe not every spirit, but try the spirits whether they are of God: because many false prophets Are gone out into the world. Hereby know you the spirit of God: Every spirit that confesses that Jesus Christ is come in the flesh is of God.

(John 4:1-2)

And every .spirit that confesses not that Jesus Christ is come in the flesh is not of God: and this is that spirit of anti-Christ, whereof you have heard that it should come; And even now already is it in the world.

(1John 4:3)

For many deceivers are entered into the world, who confess not that Christ is come in the flesh. This is a deceiver and an antichrist.

(2 John 1:7)

FOOLS

HATE

KNOWLEDGE

(Proverbs 1:22)

MY PEOPLE ARE

DESTROYED FOR

LACK OF

KNOWLEDGE (GODLY KNOWLEDGE)

(Hosea 4:6)

WHAT IS YOUR POSITION?

AS

THE WORLD
REFORM AND CONFORM

TRUE BELIEVERS
MUST

INFORM

AND

TRANSFORM

NO HUMAN

-DIVISION-

YOU

ARE

(ALL ONE)

IN

CHRIST

JESUS

(Galatians 3:28)

NONE OTHER NAME GIVEN

UNDER HEAVEN AMONG MEN FOR

MANKIND'S SALVATION

(Acts 4:12)

LOVE, TRUTH & GOODNESSS

-NOURISH-
The
HEART, MIND AND SOUL

THE WAYS
OF
RIGHTEOUSNESS

ARE

THE WAYS
OF
HAPPINESS

PROACTIVE JUSTICE

MINIMIZES

CORRUPTION &

DESTRUCTION

COMPROMISE WITH EVIL FORSAKES GOD -BETRAYS SELF & HUMANITY

Unrighteousness
Hatred
Injustice
Arrogance

VIOLATE
AND
DAMAGE

The Human Enterprise

CULTURAL COMMONALITIES And COMPATIBILITIES

ENHANCE

HUMAN LIFE'S POTENTIALITIES & POSSIBILITIES

PROACTIVE LOVE

-PREVENTS-

REACTIVE HATRED

WISDOM SHOULD

COME WITH AGE

IT IS SO SAD

WHEN AGE
COMES ALONE

ATHEISTIC LEADERSHIP & INFLUENCE DEGRADE HUMANITY And MOCK GOD

The Public Theologian

PUBLIC OFFICE SELF-SERVING RULERS

MUST BE REPLACED WITH

PUBLIC SERVING

REPRESENTATIVES

WE, THE PEOPLE

MUST TAKE A STAND
FOR
SOCIAL JUSTICE
RELIGIOUS LIBERTY
AND
TRUE DEMOCRACY
NOW!

The Public Theologian

LAWYERS AND JUDGES

DEVOID
OF BIBLICAL KNOWLEDGE

ARE NOT COMPETENT

TO ADMINISTER

EQUITABLE JUSTICE
The Public Theologian

TOLERANCE

FOR EVIL & INJUSTICE

COMPROMISES & JEOPARDIZES

THE SOUL

The Public Theologian

A
Resolution For
MANDATED, JUST,
STANDARDIZED
PROFESSIONAL
ETHICS
In All U. S. A.
GOVERNMENT
AGENCIES

But let judgment run down as waters and righteousness as a mighty stream. (Amos 5:24)

Chapter 7

Blessings of God's Word

JESUS CHRIST IS THE CENTER OF WORLD HISTORY

For other foundation can no man lay than that laid, which is Jesus Christ. (1Corinthians 3:11)

I am Alpha and Omega, the beginning and the ending, saith the Lord, which is, and which was, and which is to come, the Almighty. (Revelations 1:8)

TRUTH IS NOT RELATIVE
JUSTICE IS NOT ARBITRARY
GOD'S RIGHTEOUSNESS IS REQUIRED
EVERY SOUL IS SUBJECT UNTO GOD
LOVE GOD AND MAN ARE COMMANDMENTS

God gives you the free autonomy to represent yourself for good or bad or true or false. God is already represented in CREATION, THE BIBLE AND JESUS CHRIST.

THERE ARE PENALTIES AND DETRIMENTAL CONSEQUENCES WHEN YOU MISREPRESENT GOD, JESUS CHRIST, THE BIBLE, THE CHURCH, THE HOLY SPIRIT AND THE TRUTH.

YOUR SHEEP CLOTHING ARE TRANSPARENT TO GOD AND DISCERNING SPIRITS. GOD'S WILL IS MADE KNOWN IN HIS CREATION, HIS WORD AND HIS CHRIST. GOD DECLARES CREATION AS GOOD AND HIS PLEASURE IN HIS SON, JESUS!

THE GREATEST VALUE IS LOVE.
GOD IS LOVE.

Beloved, let us love one another: for love is of God; and everyone that loveth is born of God, and knows God. He that loveth not knoweth not God; for God is love. (1John 4:7-8)

If a man say, I love God, and hateth his brother, he is a liar: for he that loveth not his brother whom he has seen, how can he love God whom he has not seen? (1John 4:20)

A new commandment I give unto you, That ye love one another; as I have loved you, that you also love one another. (John 13:34)

LOVE
HEALS
RESTORES
NOURISHES
&
SUSTAINS

And now abideth faith, hope, love, these three, but the greatest of these is love. (1Corinthians 13:13)

THE WAY
THE TRUTH
THE LIFE
THE LIGHT
ARE
AVAILABLE

I am the light of the world: he that followeth me shall not walk in darkness, but shall have the light of life.

(John 8:12}

I am the way, the truth and the life: no man cometh to the Father, but by me.

(John 14:6)

SOCIAL PRACTICES THAT MISLEAD DECEIVE & CONFUSE ARE DETRIMENTAL TO HUMAN, MENTAL & SPIRITUAL HEALTH

There is a way which seemeth right unto a man, but the end thereof are the ways of death. (Proverbs 16:25)

DEMONIC-IDEOLOGIES (They)

DENY REALITY

DISTORT TRUTH

DESTROY LIFE

The thief cometh not, but for to steal, and to kill, and to destroy; I am come that they might have life, and that they might have it more abundantly.

(John 10:10)

The American School Choice: Make All Public Success Schools

EVIL AND IGNORANCE ARE THE GREATEST PERILS TO HUMAN LIF~E AND EXISTENCE -(SELF EVIDENT)

For we wrestle not against flesh and blood, but against principalities, against powers, against the rulers of the darkness of this world, against spiritual wickedness in high places. Wherefore take unto you the whole armour of God, that you may be able to withstand in the evil day, and having done all, to stand. (Ephesians 6:12-13)

When wisdom entereth into thine heart, and knowledge is pleasant to thine soul; Discretion shall preserve thee, understanding shall keep thee; to deliver thee from the way of the evil man, from the man that speaketh froward things. (Proverbs 2:10-12)

INJUSTICE CREATES EXPLOSIVE RAGE AND INDIGNATION

I hate, I despise your feast days, and I will not smell in your solemn assemblies. Though you offer me burnt offerings and your meat offerings, I will not accept them: neither will I regard the peace offerings of your fat beasts. Take thou away from me the noise of thy songs: for I will not hear the melody of thy viols. But let judgment run down as waters, and righteousness as a mighty stream. (Amos 21- 24).

For you have turned judgment into gall, and the fruit of righteousness into Hemlock. (Amos 6:12)

Be not deceived, God is not mocked: Whatsoever a man soweth, that shall he also reap. (Amos 6:12)

FALSE DOCTRINES THAT MISEDUCATE, MISLEAD AND ABUSE CHILDREN ARE ABOMINATIONS

For they being ignorant of God's righteousness, and going about to establish their own righteousness, have not submitted themselves unto the righteousness of God. (Romans 10:3)

Woe unto them that call evil good, and good evil; that put darkness for light, and light for darkness; that put bitter for sweet and sweet for bitter! (Isaiah 5:20)

And whosoever shall offend one of these little ones that believe in me, it is better for him that a millstone were hanged about his neck, and he were cast into the sea. (Mark 9:42)

THOSE WHO ABUSE FREEDOM FORFEIT THEIR ENTITLEMENT TO ITS BLESSINGS

Yea, they are greedy dogs which can never have enough, and they are shepherds that cannot understand: they all look to their own way, everyone for his gain, from his quarter. (Isaiah 56:11)

For the love of money is the root of all evil: which while some coveted after, they have erred from the faith, and pierced them -selves through with many sorrows. (1Timothy 6:10)

The United States
Of America
A
National Affirmation
Of
The Biblical Word
The Savior Christ
The Creator God

Let every soul be subject unto the higher powers. For there is no power but of God: the powers that be are ordained of God.

(Romans 13:1)

RESOLVED CONFIRMATION

HUMAN LIFE IS SACRED FROM GOD AND PURPOSED BY GOD

So God created man in his own image, in the image of God created he him; male and female created he them. And God blessed them, and God said unto them, be fruitful, and multiply, and replenish the earth, and subdue it; and have dominion over the fish of the sea and over the fowl of the air, and over every living thing that moves upon the earth.

(Genesis 1:28)

UNITED STATES OF AMERICA

NATIONAL RESOLVED AFFIRMATION

IN GOD WE TRUST

Blessed is the nation whose God is the Lord; and the people whom he has chosen for his own inheritance.

(Psalm 33:12)

THOSE WHO OPPOSE THE WILL OF GOD AND THE RIGHTS OF MAN MUST BE DEFEATED!!!

But woe unto you, scribes and pharisees, hypocrites! For ye shut up the kingdom of heaven against men: for ye neither go in yourselves neither suffer ye them that are entering to go in. (Matthew 23:13)

Beware of false prophets, which come to you in sheep's clothing, but inwardly they are ravening wolves. (Matthew 7:15)

THE WILL OF GOD AND GOD GIVEN HUMAN RIGHTS MUST PREVAIL

For God so loved the world that he gave his only begotten Son, that whosoever believe in him should not perish but have everlasting life. (John 3:16)

The spirit of the Lord is upon me, because he has anointed me to preach the gospel to the poor; he has sent me to heal the brokenhearted, to preach deliverance to the captives and recovering of sight to the blind, to set at liberty them that are bruised. (Luke 4:18)

IN CHRIST
YOU ARE
NO MORE STRANGERS
NO MORE FOREIGNERS
NO MORE ALIENS
BUT
FELLOW CITIZENS
IN THE
HOUSEHOLD OF GOD

Now therefore you are no more strangers and foreigners, but fellow citizens with the saints, and of the household of God (Ephesians 2:19)

RENDER TO ALL THEIR DUES OWE NO MAN ANY THING

LOVE ONE ANOTHER

Render therefore to all their dues: tribute to whom tribute is due; custom to whom custom; fear to whom fear; honor to whom honor (Romans 13:7).

Owe no man anything, but to love one another: for he that loveth another has fulfilled the law (Romans 13:8).

THE COURAGE AND THE FAITH TO LIVE

IN THE FACE OF THREATS AND DANGER

For whosoever will save his life shall lose it: and whosoever shall lose his life for my sake, shall find it (Matthew 16:25).

When the wicked, even mine enemies and my foes, came upon me to eat up my flesh, they stumbled and fell. Though an host should encamp against me, my heart shall not fear: though war should rise against me, in this will I be confident (Psalm 27:2-3).

LOVE
GOODNESS, TRUTH, BEAUTY, HOPE, FAITH, MERCY, KNOWLEDGE, WISDOM AND UNDER -STANDING

NOURISH & SUSTAIN THE HEART, MIND, SOUL AND BODY

I am the bread of life: he that cometh to me shall never hunger; and he that believeth on me shall never thirst (John 6:35)

ONE HUMANITY ONE IN CHRIST

There is neither Jew nor Greek, there is neither bond nor free, there is neither male nor female: for you are all one in. Christ Jesus. And if you be Christ's, then are you Abraham's seed, and heirs according to the promise (Galatians 3:28- 29).

God's Commandment to warn the wicked for your vindication

"When I say unto the wicked, you shall surely die; and you give him not warning, nor speak to warn the wicked from his wicked way, to save his life; the same wicked man shall die in his iniquity; but his blood will I require at your hand."

(Ezekiel 3:18-19)

God's Commandment to Warn the Righteous to Vindicate Yourself

"Again, when a righteous man does turn from his righteousness, and commit iniquity, and I lay a stumbling block before him, he shall die: because you have not given him warning, he shall die in his sin, and his righteousness which he has done shall not be remembered; but his blood will I require at your hand."

(Ezekiel 3:20-21)

JESUS CHRIST THE ETERNAL I AM

- I am that bread of life (Jn 6:48).
- I am the living bread which came down from heaven (Jn 6:51).
- I am the light of the world (Jn 8:12).
- I am from above. I am not of this world (Jn 8:23).
- Jesus said unto them •.. Before Abraham was, I am (Jn 8:58).
- I am the good shepherd (Jn 10:11).
- I am the true vine and my Father is the husband man (Jn 15:1).
- I am the vine, ye are the branches (Jn 15:5).
- I am the resurrection, and the life(Jn 11:25).
- I am Alpha and Omega, the beginning and end (Jn 22:13).
- I am the root and the offspring of David (Rv 22:16)
- Fear not, I am the first and the last: I am he that liveth, and was dead; and behold, I am alive forevermore, Amen (Rv 1:17).

ABSOLUTE SECURITY IN JESUS CHRIST\

For I am persuaded that neither death, nor life, nor angels, nor principalities, nor powers, nor things present, nor things to come,

Nor height nor depth, nor any other creature, shall be able to separate us from the love of God, which is in Christ Jesus our lord. (Romans 8:38-39)

For God so loved the world, that he gave his only begotten Son, that whosoever believe in him should not perish, but have everlasting life. (John 3:16)

A PEOPLE WITH THE LAWS OF GOD AND THE MIND OF CHRIST INSCRIBED IN THEIR HEARTS AND MINDS

For this is the covenant that I will make with the house of Israel after those days, saith the Lord; I will put my laws into their mind, and write them in their hearts: and I will be to them a God, and they shall be to me a people.

(Hebrews 8:10)

For who has known the mind of the Lord, that he may instruct him? But we have the mind of Christ.

(1 Corinthians 2:16)

Let this mind be in you, which was also in Christ Jesus.

(Philippians 2:5)

SALVATION IN GOD'S KINGDOM REQUIRES A NEW BIRTH

Jesus answered and said unto him, verily, verily1 I say unto thee1 Except a man be born again1 he cannot see the kingdom of God.

(John 3:3)

Therefore if any man be in Christ1 he is a new creature: old things are passed away; behold, all things are become new. And all things are of God1 who has reconciled us to himself by Jesus Christ, and has given to us the ministry of reconciliation.

(2Corinthians 5:17-18)

And as we have borne the image of the earthy, we shall also bear the image of the heavenly.

(1Corinthians 15:49)

Chapter 8

Contextualizing Religion and Biblical Scripture

There is much confusion about the definition and meaning of religion in relationship to the Bible. The Bible and religion are not synonymous. Religion is construed as a very broad terminology. This broad concept of religion encompasses various sectarian, cultic and other philosophical and ideological belief systems and practices. The broad perspective of religion includes the recognized world religions and other lesser known belief systems of worship. This broad terminology and use of religion has evolved into the inclusion of things and ideas that are even antithetical to the traditional concepts of religion. This broad use of religion words, the broad use of religion does not require a belief in God. This broad use of religion can and often does include atheistic believers. This all inclusiveness of religion has been reinforced by the U. S. Supreme Court under the Establishment Clause of the First Amendment which prohibits an establishment of religion. The Supreme Court goes further in its rulings using the broad interpretation of religion. It "equates" all religions. Additionally, the Supreme Court equates the religious and the nonreligious.

This broad view and interpretation of religion without a substantive or operational definition of true and valid religion, create confusion and nullify the intended benefits and blessings of the traditional concepts of religion. The confusion of religion and the equality of all religions create confusion about the religious creeds and texts of the various religions. This relegated equality of all religions and subsequently their religious creeds precipitates their irrelevance and diminish their humanitarian value. This is the ultimate subordination and marginalization of religion. When considering this subordination and marginalization of religion it is understandable how the U. S. Supreme Court and other lower courts have outlawed prayer and religious education in the public schools and other governmental establishments. This broad use and view of religion have been used to make important decisions that have impacted detrimentally in the lives, institutions and cultural values of the American society and beyond. Due to these decisions based on the indefinite and nebulous use of religion have deprived the American people and world civilization of the most advanced moral, ethical and civilized humanitarian standards known to mankind. This dilution, corruption and degeneration of cultural survival values have happened and continues to happen because the Bible and the Judea-Christian values and faith have been erroneously labeled and considered to be a religion. The erroneous labeling the Bible as a religion subjects it to the First Amendment that reads, "Congress shall make no law respecting an establishment of religion, or prohibiting the free exercise thereof: or abridging the freedom of speech, or of the press; or the right of the people peaceably to assemble, and to petition the Government for a redress of grievance."

The following accounts about the Bible and scriptural references of the Bible will clearly indicate that the Bible is not a religion and biblical education is not a religion. According to biblical authorities, the Old Testament contains 37 books. The first 5 books of the Bible; namely; Genesis, Exodus, Leviticus, Numbers and Deuteronomy are **LAW** books. Twelve books of the Old Testament are classified as **HISTORY**. They are known as Joshua, Judges, Ruth! Samuel, 2Samuel, IKing, 2King, !Chronicles, 2Chronicles, Ezra, Nehemiah and Esther. Five books of the Old Testament are classified as **POETRY or WISDOM** books. These books are known as, Job, Psalms, Proverbs, Ecclesiastes and Solomon's Song. The five books known as Isaiah, Jeremiah, Lamentations, Ezekiel and Daniel are known as **MAJOR PROPHETS**. There are twelve books of the Old Testament known as **MINOR PROPHETS**. They are Hosea, Joel, Amos, Obadiah, Jonah, Micah, Nahum, Habakkuk, Zephaniah, Haggai, Zechariah and Malachi Please notice that no book of these 37 books of the Old Testament is classified as religion. These books have definite titles and classifications. The nebulous and confusing word religion is not mentioned. God is not a God of confusion. The twenty- seven New Testament books consist of the following titles or categories: Four **GOSPELS**, known as Matthew, Mark, Luke and John. One **HISTORY** Book known as Acts; 14 books of **LETTERS**, entitled Romans, !Corinthians, 2Corinthians, Galatians, Ephesians, Philippians, Colossians, !Thessalonians, 2Thessalonians, !Timothy, 2Timothy, Titus, Philemon, Hebrews, James, IPeter, 2Peter, IJohn, 2John, 3John and Jude. The last book of the New Testament is under the title or category of **PROPHECY**. The last book is Revelation. Again, these books in the New Testament, as is the case of the Old Testament, do not carry the title or mention religion. The book of Acts is the **CHURCH HISTORY** book. Church would be the closest connotation to religion. However, religion is not mentioned in any of the biblical books categories or titles. It is mystifying how religion could become such an impactful word in society, the government and the courts of law in America with no biblical prominence. The most significant aspect of the Bible and its 66 books, is that the bible is the revelatory WORD of GOD that offers SALVATION for mankind. The Bible declares in Acts 4:12: "Neither is there salvation in any other: for there is none other name under heaven given among men, whereby we must be saved." Is there any authority among men in the annals of history that can dispute God's salvation gift in Acts 4:12? Let it be noted that this salvation of God for mankind is not found in the government, the nation, the bank, the Church nor religion. John 3:16 provides the answer: "For God so loved the world,that he gave his only Begotten Son, that whosoever believeth in him should not perish, but have everlasting life." Salvation is in God's SON. As lofty as the holy places of cities, mountains, cathedrals, temples and sanctuaries, feasts and religions, renown saints, prophets and priests, God's salvation is not there. SALVATION IS IN THE SON. The Bible contains the good news and gospel of salvation. How awful it is to deprive God's children and God's people of this GOOD NEWS OF SALVATION FROM GOD. It is an urgent and top priority to remove this confusion about religion and bring clarity and accessibility to Bible teaching and Bible education to all God's children.

The purpose of the enumerations of the book titles in the Bible is to gain some understanding about how the nebulous terminology of religion incorporated and coopted the Bible and biblical education. This cooption of the Bible and biblical education into religion has been grossly misleading, damaging and tragic. It has brought about the legal prohibition and deprivation of biblical education and prayer in the public schools and other government domains. There is an erroneous presumption in the interpretation of the Establishment Clause of the First Amendment that the Bible is a religion.

The Bible, nor biblical education, is a religion or establishment of religion as presumed by the interpretation of the Establishment Clause of the First Amendment. The Bible is very definitive. It speaks for itself. Each Testament, Book, Chapter and Bible Verse in the Bible speak for itself. The theologians have advanced two methods of explaining Biblical Scriptures. One method is known as, "exegesis." Exegesis means to accept the literal words and thoughts expressed by the language used. The second method is known as, "eisegesis." Eisegesis means to insert one's own opinions or interpretation of the Scripture that may be different from the literal rendering of the particular

Scripture. Even the eisegesis method will allow the comparison of what is written and what is interpreted. The final books of the Bible were canonized in the 4th Century A.D. No manmade authority is authorized to make any changes in the Bible. It is a closed book for all time. Nothing can be added and nothing can be taken away. Even after two thousand years, the message of the Bible is as relevant or more so in the 20th Century than ever before. All barriers, legalities, worldliness, ignorance and arrogance must be removed to allow the most significant, urgent and vital message from God to mankind to get through, unimpeded, to starving minds, hearts and souls. It is incredible that the Nation of America, as a "Nation under God," has allowed the greatest message to mankind to be blocked by the use and cooption of the word, religion, by a manmade statutory law in a nation with a motto that says, "In God We Trust." The misuse of religion by an uninformed Court of Law in a Nation blessed by God, has deprived generation of students and millions of people the greatest, oldest and most enduring vital human knowledge of all history and time.

The Bible is not a secret. It is the best- known book and best- selling book of all history. It is the greatest classical literature of all history. It is the unique book of history. It is the book that reveals God's revelation of himself, his love, his will and his Son of salvation to the world. How could such a book be prohibited in public schools or any place where people inhabit? How can and how could this deprivation be accepted by so many people? Sunday and other days of the week are set aside in churches and other places of worship. How could these millions of people be indifferent to the deprivation of this vital knowledge for our children and the oncoming generations in the public -school systems and other government establishments? These questions are raised to help us to wake up and come to ourselves and our senses and the awareness of God's gifts and his manifested love for humanity. The Bible is not a religion or bad thing to avoid; it is a God inspired vital life saving message to be embraced by all people and all generations everywhere

Heterogeneous cultural diversity, mental and spiritual disordered hatred and misguided technology is an omnibus threat and danger to humanity and civilization. The Bible is the blueprint for human life and human survival. Those who want to embrace life and live must awake from their irresponsible indifference and slumbering stupor; embrace and proclaim the Biblical Word of God as never before. The believers in God must become full time advocates, teachers, practitioners and proclaimers of God's Word. The believers must realize the danger of people who do not know the word of God in the Bible. God's Biblical Word must be shared in every home and to every child and person. In a technological world, the lethal risk to humanity is too great to be and live in the midst of people who are devoid of the Biblical Word of God. Biblical education must become a top priority in all educational institutions. It is unwise and even absurd to employ teachers, administrators or elect or appoint public officials who are atheistic and devoid of the knowledge of God and the love of Jesus Christ. Sin, wickedness and evil are lethal threats to humanity. The technological age has forced believers and responsible humanity to become one household of faith. Humanity must become one family. Those who are disobedient, rebellious and alien to the will of God must be separated. Some may entertain the idea that this is cruel. This is taking responsibility to survive. Jesus said (Matthew 5:29-30) 11If thy right eye offend thee, pluck it out, and cast it from thee And if thy right hand offend thee, cut it off, ad cast it from thee ... for it is profitable for thee that one of thy members should perish and not thy whole body should be cast into hell." America, humanity, families and individuals are in a place where hard choices must be made. The human predicament in the technological age requires unpleasant major extricating surgery and radical healing, restoring courage, faith and love medical and spiritual therapy. It requires the healing balm of Gilead. It requires putting on the whole armor of God. It requires the faith that can move mountains. It requires the love that never fails. It requires a decision to trust in God. It requires a decision to choose life in Christ.

Tragically, the judicial decisions of the courts have used an undefined definition of religion that surreptitiously ignored or mischaracterized the Bible and biblical education. The indefinite broad use of religion has been erroneously used to deny biblical and theological education in public schools under a faulty presumption that the Bible is a religion or that it represents an establishment of religion. The broad inclusive undefined use of religion is unclear and confusing. The presumptions based on this unclear, broad definition and use of religion are invalid and at best, are misguided. The broad unclear definition of religion and subsequent presumptions have deprived, and many instances, have legalized the prohibition of the Bible and biblical education. These legal decisions to prohibit biblical education and the presumed religious symbols in public institutions and in the public square are doing great harm to the culture and humanity. The message of the Bible speaks for itself. THE BIBLE SPEAKS FOR ITSELF The Bible is its own authority. It speaks for itself. It speaks on more subjects about human life, the earth and the creation than any other volume. It speaks very little about religion. According to James Strong's Exhaustive Bible Concordance, the Bible makes seven references to religion. The book of Acts has two references to religion: (Acts 13:43}, (Acts 26:5); two references in Galatians: (Galatians 1:13, 1:14); three references in the book of James: (1:26, 1:26, 1:27); Based on this sparse reference to religion in the Bible, it must be concluded that religion is scarcely used in the Bible.

A BRIEF SUMMARY OF BIBLICAL SCRIPTURAL REFERENCES

James Strong's Bible Concordance contains relevant and enlightening biblical references about voluminous subjects of the Bible. These subjects relate to timeless human values. An exploration of these biblical subjects and human values provide valuable information in determining the basic themes and subject matter of the Bible. This information is provided to refute the erroneous presumptions that the Bible or biblical knowledge is a religion. It is provided additionally, to refute the erroneous claim, that the Bible or biblical education in public schools and other government domains, violate the Establishment Clause of the First Amendment of the U. S. Constitution. These Scriptural references provide overwhelming evidence and infallible proof that the Bible is not a religion and is not synonymous to religion. These Scriptural references will also reveal the great forfeitures and invaluable benefits lost .by outlawing the Bible in public schools. This legal deprivation of the Biblical education in public schools and other government domains have robbed the American culture of invaluable knowledge, refinement and enrichment. The conclusions that the Bible or biblical knowledge does not belong in public education, public life and the public square is a drastic departure from the world of reality and the foundational values that made America an exceptional nation under God. To be as succinct as possible, only Scriptural references and respective numbers of occurrences will be enumerated. These selected Scriptural references relate to human beings, their institutions, their values, their government, their families, their freedom, their leaders, their nations, the earth and God. **BIBLICAL SCRIPTURES DEFINING ROLES OF HUMAN FAMILIES:** The Bible has 2603 references to **MAN**. It has a greater number for **MEN** in the Concordance Appendix. The Bible has 539 references to **WOMAN** and **WOMEN**. The Bible has 71 references to the **WOMAN'S WOMB**. It has 395 references to **FAMILIES**. The Bible has 200 references to **CHILD** and 1778 references to CHILDREN. The Bible has 251 references to **MOTHER AND MOTHERS**. It has 963 references to **FATHER** and a greater number in the Concordance Appendix for **FATHERS, FATHER'S AND FATHERS.**' The Bible has 363 references to **BROTHER** and 109 to **SISTER**. There are 106 references to the single and plurality of **HUSBAND**. There are 532 references to the singular and plurality of **WIFE AND WIVES. SCRIPTURAL REFERENCES TO WORSHIP:** The Bible has 108 Scriptural references to WORSHIP, 71 to **WORSHIPPED,** two to **WORSHIPPER,** 7 to **WORSHIPPERS**. 6 to **WORSHIPPETH** and 5 to **WORSHIPPING.** Many of these worshipping references include idol worship. Although the Bible represents Jewish History with a monotheistic belief in one God; the Gentiles and other nations, many of whom worshipped many different gods, a practice known as polytheism. Objects of things worshipped are wide ranged from the Godly to the ungodly. There is also the reality of false religions.

The Bible is the most inclusive book of the world of reality and the expressions of the abiding varieties of human nature. The Bible includes the good and the bad; the holy and the unholy; the truth and deceptions. There is an unbiased and objectivity in the Bible that transcends the nature and wisdom of mankind. It is a book of human history where God intervened and revealed his love and his plan of salvation for mankind. It is puzzling that such a vital body and document of knowledge would be so widely rejected and prohibited. Religion is nebulous, general and indefinite. These biblical references are clear, definite, quantitative and numerically classified. The nature, age, durability, relevance, specificity and authority of the Bible are voluminous manifestations of its validity and authenticity. It cannot be connotated with religion. It transcends human institutions, cultures, religions and statutory laws. It is a revelation and visitation from above. **BIBLICAL SCRIPTURES OF HUMAN VALUES**: The Bible contains 174 references to **TRUTH;** 106 references to **UNDERSTAND;** 160 to **UNDERSTANDING; 37 to UNDERSTOOD;** 233 references to **WISDOM;** 247 to WISE; 71 references to **REASON;** 12 references to **REASONED;** 5 references to **REASONING,** 2 to **REASONS;** 19 to **BALANCING**. The book of Proverbs along with other books of the Bible are known as wisdom books. The Bible itself, has been described as the "Wisdom of the Ages." It is an ongoing human tragedy that millions and billions of people on the earth are born and they die not having learned the most significant, precious and vital salvation knowledge revealed to mankind. The most massive minds of men have studied and perused the Biblical Scriptures for over two thousand years; and they have not been able to add to its completeness and take away from its richness. The Bible is the only complete book that needs no revisions, updates, additions nor subtractions. It has been inspired and authorized by God. The Bible is its own authority. No man or manmade authority is authorized to add or take away from this complete **BOOK OF LIFE.**

SCRIPTURAL REFERENCES TO ULTIMATE HUMAN LIFE VALUES: The Bible has 442 references to **LIFE**. It has 552 references to LOVE; 75 references to BEAUTY and hundreds of references to **GOOD** and **GOODNESS** in the Exhaustive Bible Concordance Appendix. The Bible addresses universal human values for all people, generations and nations throughout the earth. It is perplexing and disappointing to observe how the greatest human values known to mankind, could be so marginalized and minimized in society's major institutions of families, churches, schools, businesses, governments, commerce and nations. This must change for the sake of human survival. There is an urgency to resurrect, prioritize, proclaim, embrace, teach and practice these vital God given human values with utmost seriousness, commitment and diligence.

BIBLICAL REFERENCES TO LAW AND GOVERNANCE:

It is a tragic irony and revelation that the very designated institution in society that teach, practice and administer the laws and justice, ignore and disregard the original and foundational laws of the Bible. The overwhelming majority of American law schools do not include the Bible or theological courses in their curriculum. This blatant exclusion of the Bible and theology from the education, administration and practice of law in the executive, legislative, judicial branches of government and the public society in general; is symptomatic of an ungrateful, rebellious, secular and atheistic society. This is an alarming indication that the American Government and the American society have strayed away from its foundational principles and values rooted in the Judea-Christian Bible. America cannot survive by forsaking its Pledge as, "A Nation Under God," its Motto, "In God We Trust," and the "Evidentiary Truths," and, "Unalienable Rights •. Equality, Life, Liberty and Pursuit of Happiness," of the Declaration of Independence ordained by God. This straying away or moving away from the founding creeds of the Judea-Christian Bible is evidenced by the U. S. Courts using manmade statutory laws to override the Divine and natural laws. These manmade statutory laws prohibit Bible teaching and prayer in public schools and other government facilities. There have been statutory laws prohibiting Bibles in hotel rooms, crosses on public property and even in cemeteries. The Ten Commandments have been forbidden in court rooms. There are prohibitions against Christian music in public schools and other government establish!'flents. There are prohibitions against saying "Merry Christmas" at Christmas time. Some public officials refuse to use the Bible to be sworn in to public office. The Nativity Scene is forbidden on government establishments. The U. S. Courts have ruled that all religions are on an equal plane. One religion cannot be favored over another religion. Even atheistic believers are on the same equal plane with believers. Persons who do not believe in God have equal rights with believers. However, this contradicts America's Pledge as, "One Nation under God," and its Motto as inscribed on the coins and currency as, "In God We Trust," and the," evidentiary truths endowed by God," and the "Unalienable rights of life, liberty and. the pursuit of happiness." Of the Declaration of Independence. God declares his people as a chosen generation, a royal priesthood, an holy nation, a peculiar people who have been delivered from darkness to his marvelous light. All of America's creeds acknowledge God. The Bible is the Book and Message of God.

This moving away from the truths of the Bible in the American culture is a tragic deceptive misguided willful ignorance. It is a kind of dogmatic ignorance. It is willful and passionate. It is a passionate unwillingness to explore, examine and to analyze the evidence and merits of the Bible. It is a bias based on wishful thinking, assumptions and preconceived biased concepts. There are self- deceptive motives and assumptions to dismiss the significance of the Bible by lumping it into the nebulous concept of the indefinite terminology of religion. There are self- deceptive reasons for believing that the Bible has no value and consequently, the decision turns into an assumption that it (the Bible) has no real or significant meaning. Therefore, it is easily dismissed, ignored, demeaned, belittled and outlawed. The deprivation of biblical knowledge in the American culture or any culture has cultural degenerative detrimental consequences. The progression of the cultural, moral and ethical degeneration is leading to societal destabilization and destruction. This writing is an appeal, a request, a petition and a plea to ministers, churches, leaders, public officials and believers in God and all citizens and patriotic persons to join forces to get this biblical knowledge and education back into the homes, families, churches, schools, government, cultures and nations to civilize human beings, save humanity, enrich, enlighten and refine human cultures.

THE BIBLE AS A BOOK OF LAW:

The first five books of the Bible: Genesis, Exodus, Leviticus. Numbers and Deuteronomy are classified as Law Books of the Bible. These are not nebulous books of religion. They are books of laws that establish the laws and the guidelines for regulating human behavior for individuals, families, communities, leaders, governments and nations. In addition to these five books, there are numerous Scriptural references to LAW in the Bible. The James Strong Bible Concordance provides 605 Scriptural references to LAW, 39 for LAWFUL, 20 for LAWS and 7 Scriptural references for LAWYERS. There are 10 Scriptural references for EQUITY, 26 for LIBERTY, 39 for MERCIFUL and 276 references for MERCY. In addition to LAW, the Bible is rich in resources of JUSTICE. There are 91 Scriptural references to JUST, 28 for JUSTICE, 206 for JUDGMENT, 333 for JUDGMENTS and 52 references for JUDGES, 189 references for JUDGE and 80 references for JUDGED. As is presented, the Bible has an abundance of information and knowledge about LAW, JUSTICE, JUDGES, JUDGMENTS and JUDICIAL ADMINISTRATION along with associated references of LAWYERS and GOVERNMENT. This abundance of knowledge about law, Lawyers, Judges, Justice and the administration of Justice in the Bible; add to the perplexing puzzle as to how this original foundational judicial information and knowledge could be ignored by the law schools, the courts, the governments, society and the American "Nation Under God?" The moral compass and the foundational truths of the Bible have not moved, nor changed. However, this tragic separation and disparity between the American Government and American people and culture have moved away from this life giving anchored, unchanging source of God, the BIBLE.

The BIBLE is the inexhaustible life source book for all mankind. In bringing these brief Scriptural references to a close, the Bible has much to say about leaders and leadership. It has 2150 references to KING. It has 392 references to KINGDOMS. It has 477 references to NATIONS. The Bible has 982 references to EARTH. Contemplate what JOB said 700 years before the coming of Jesus Christ in Job 26:7, "He stretches out the north over the empty place, and he hangs the earth upon nothing." There are a number of references where God Shakes the heaven and the earth. How awesome were these God inspired minds before the coming of Christ and the advent of science, that prehistoric people could contemplate the shaking of the heavens and the earth. The treasures and wonders of the Bible are wanting for exploration and discovery. It is the most exciting and fascinating document in existence. The Bible has 984 Scriptural references to JESUS and 554 to CHRIST. There are 164 Scriptural references to SALVATION that JESUS CHRIST brings. JESUS CHRIST IS THE SOLE INDIVIDUAL IN THE BIBLE AND IN HISTORY TO BECOME THE EVENT THAT DIVIDES ISTORY IN BC (Before Christ) and AD (In the year of our Lord). When Jesus Came, the calendar custodians started counting backwards from his birth to the past, and forward from his birth to the future. JESUS CHRIST IS THE INDELIBLE EVENT THAT DIVIDED HISTORY INTO BC AND AD. EACH USE AND RECOGNITION OF CALENDAR DATES IS AN ACKNOWLEDGEMENT OF THE COMING OF JESUS CHRIST IN HISTORY ON THE PLANET EARTH. HE BIBLE IS THE INCOMPARABLE AND UNIQUE BOOK OF GOD'S CREATION, REVELATION AND SALVATION. NO, THE BIBLE IS NOT ABOUT THE NEBULOUS TERMINOLOGY OF RELIGION. THE BIBLE HAS 4350 REFERENCES TO GOD. THERE ARE 7981 REFERENCES TO LORD IN THE BIBLE. IF ONE SUBJECT ABOUT THE BIBLE IS CHOSEN, IT WOULD BE THE SUBJECT, THE OBJECT AND LOVE OF GOD IN JESUS CHRIST. FOR ANYONE TO DENY OR IGNORE THE REALITY AND TRUTHS OF THE BIBLE; IT WOULD REQUIRE THE SELLING OF ONE'S SOUL, LEAPING FROM LIGHT TO THE HADES OF DARKNESS AND PLUNGING ONE'S SELF INTO THE ABYSMAL SEA OF MENTAL INSANITY AND THE HELL OF SPIRITUAL SUICIDE. "How shall we escape, if we neglect so great salvation." (Hebrews 2:3) This new enlightening light shed on the Bible in relationship to the confusion about the definition, role and misuse of religion, must be shared with all leaders and administrators in the American Government from the National, State and local municipalities. It must be shared with all clergy, educators and citizens. This vital knowledge of the Bible must be taught, preached and assimilated in all institutions, communities, individuals and groups. It is the duty of the blessed America and Nation under God to share this GOOD NEWS WITH THE WHOLE WORLD!

BIBLICAL THEOLOGICAL VISION PERSPECTIVE
(Focused Discernment for Biblical Truth)

A serious, faithful, and spiritual study of the Bible will reveal the revelations of God's Will. God's Biblical revelations will include, (1) Valid Principles for living, (2) Sound Doctrines for true knowledge and understanding, (3) Abiding Truths to believe to teach and to live by, (4) God's instructions and commandments for mankind to live by, (5) Man's willful disobedience and rebellion against God, and (6) the Love of God for mankind. The Bible provides the clearest revelation of the human nature of man in relationship to mankind and God. A loving God who knows man and loves man provides clear instructions for man to live according to the Will of God to get the most out of life. life is the supreme Value according to God's Word in the Bible. God's principles, sound doctrines, truths, instructions, commandments and love are designed to protect man's life; and even provide abundant and eternal life. THE BIBLE IS THE SUPREME BOOK OF LIFE. IT IS A CONTINUING PRIORITY OF THOSE VALUES FROM GOD THAT SUSTAIN HUMAN LIFE. BIBLICAL KNOWLEDGE IS THE MOST VITAL NEED OF THE 21st CENTURY. The safeguard, development, redemption and salvation are the primary themes of the Bible. Our study of God's Word is a search for values, knowledge, powers and resources to sustain this precious human life. The Biblical values represent the accumulated knowledge, wisdom and truth of the ages to understand and sustain human life. There is no other book outside the Bible with this blue print for the ultimate instructions on life and living. The contents of this Bible are over two thousand years, and yet, it is THE MOST RELEVANT BOOK FOR OUR CRISIS TIMES IN THIS 21st Century. You are invited to journey through the Bible in search of vital revelations of truths, knowledge, understanding and wisdom to redeem human life from its brink of destruction and death. Put on your eyes of faith and spirit of love.

Biblical Good News from God

The Good News of the Bible undergirds, supports, balances and authorizes all other true knowledge and education for human life to live and glorify God. The old Testament and the New Testament are Good News from God. This Gospel is for the whole person and the whole world. This Gospel is for attentive ears, to listen and learn. It is for the mind to understand, analyze, and synthesize. It is for the eyes to see and behold. It is for the heart to feel and believe. The Gospel is for the mouth and tongue to speak it, teach it, proclaim it and sing it. The Gospel is a heavenly sound and a joyful noise. The Gospel is for the feet to walk it; run it; dance it; transport and expand it throughout the world. The Gospel is for the arms and hands to reach out with it; embrace it; and serve humanity with it. The Gospel is for the mind to think it; for the heart to love it; be inspired and sing it. It is for the soul to embrace it and cherish it. The Gospel is for the believer to study it, learn it, and use it for the unfinished task of God's kingdom building on the earth. The Gospel is for the artist to paint it; to sculpt it; to write it; to chant it and to sing it with the full force of aesthetic expression. The Gospel is for the scientist to observe and practice with honesty and truth. It is for the judiciary to incorporate, legislate and mandate with justice, equity and liberty. The Gospel is for families to be instructed by it and for children to be nurtured by it. The Gospel is for communities to become allied with it and unified by it. The Gospel is for nations and governments to be guided, blessed and ruled by its righteousness, justice and mercy. The Gospel is for nations to overcome their alienations, separations and states of being foreigners, strangers and enemies; and become one nation and one human family in the household and kingdom of God. Jesus Christ is the unique best Good News to come to the earth. His birth, life, ministry, crucifixion, resurrection and ascension are Good News. All of his words and actions are Good News. Everything that was said about Jesus is Good News. Everything that was done to Jesus is Good News, including the sacrificial crucifixion. The most amazing Good News of all, is recorded by Matthew, Mark and Luke, a quote from God, "This is my Beloved Son, in whom I am well pleased." Good News about the Old Testament, the New Testament and Jesus ChristIs

GOOD NEWS FROM GOD.
The Authority for Prayer in U.S. Public Schools
It is Evil to Erect Barriers between Mankind and God

According to BIBLICAL AUTHORITY no form of government exempts mankind from the sovereignty, authority and jurisdiction of God. All people, the earth and the fullness thereof belong to God (Psalm 24:1), and subject to the power of God (Romans 13:1). ALL PEOPLE HAVE A RIGHT TO PRAY TO GOD IN SPIRIT AND IN TRUTH ANY PLACE AND AT ANY TIME. The most privileged and blessed communication known to mankind is the high sacred privilege of communicating with God. The Bible contains voluminous references, worship and communication between man and God. According to the New Strong Concordance there are over 540 references to prayer in the combined 66 Books of the Bible. No human agency or government is authorized by God to restrict any person from the sacred privilege of communicating with God. God created man in his image and likeness (Genesis 1:27-28)with the nature to love, be loved and communicate with God. Any spirit or person that seek to separate and alienate God's people from God is evil and wicked. The knowledge of God and the communication with God are so vital that every parent, child custodian and educational institution have a sacred duty to teach, train, educate and assimilate the knowledge of the Bible and the worship of God to every child. The failure to do so is tantamount to criminal negligence. Jesus Christ expressed detrimental consequences to those who offend children who believe in him in the following Scripture: "But whoso shall offend one of these little ones which believe in me, it were better for him that a millstone were hanged about his neck, and that he were drowned in the depths of the sea (Matthew 18:6)." There are many Biblical Scriptures that teach parental, educational and societal responsibilities for teaching children about God, morality and ethical responsibility. The State of Georgia has a law (Georgia Law 20-2-145) that mandates that all children from kindergarten through Twelfth

Grade be taught character education. Georgia also has another law, (20-2-148), entitled, Elective course in History and Literature of the Old and New Testaments Eras for Grades 9-12. These two laws are grossly neglected in too many public schools in Georgia. THAT MUST CHANGE! This neglect is not innocent. It is criminal. This neglect is not benign. IT IS TOXIC, EVIL AND DANGEROUS! What is more offensive and damaging to a child than depriving the child of the vital knowledge about God and the vital means of communicating and connecting with GOD through education, fellowship and prayer? Governments and all persons with influence and authority must haste to incorporate Biblical knowledge and character education in their educational curricula and the RIGHT TO PRAY AND WORSHIP GOD IN SPIRIT AND IN TRUTH IN THE DECENCY AND ORDER OF GOD AT ANY PLACE IN GOD'S CREATION! This is a high privilege, Sacred responsibility and solemn duty.

The Sacred Journey Through the Bible
Pastor W. J. Webb

The sacred journey through the Bible is more revealing and productive when you travel by faith with spiritual light and alertness to be able to see the truth, discern the spirits and recognize the authenticity and authority of the Word of God. When traveling with reverence and a purpose the journey is likely to be more rewarding. The biblical journey is a sacred and serious journey in search of messages, knowledge, answers and inspiration from God. This biblical journey highlights the reality of man's intimate relationship possibilities with the Almighty God. God's revelation and spiritual light enable and empower believers to sort out those things that hinder healthy communications and healthy relationships with man and with God. God gives spiritual insight that enables believers to be discerning of biases, prejudices, vanities, self-deceptions and hatred. God gives special insight to believers to identify and distinguish the sound, valid, credible, authentic and genuine truth of God. The study of God's Word enhances the believers ability to understand truth and sound doctrines. This significant journey through the Holy Bible is most rewarding when the spiritual traveler is mentally alert, spiritually and emotionally attuned to seek God's truth, knowledge and enlightenment. When believers seek, ask and knock with faith, hope and prayerful expectation, God will answer, fulfill and run your cup over. God promises his revelatory disclosure when a believer seeks and searches for God with the whole heart. The study of the Bible is a journey of faith. The whole intellect is used in the study of the Bible. However, it is primarily an adventure of faith. Unbelievers without faith cannot please God. Unbelievers are in a state of rebellion against God and a self-imposed ignorance and darkness. This ignorance, darkness and rebellion are impediments to the study and understanding of God's Word. Such persons are not ready for the sacred journey through the Bible. God's Biblical Word has new revelations to meet the new challenges, problems and wickedness of this generation and every generation and nation. God has a comprehensive diagnosis of man kinds problems. God is the foremost authority on the human nature of man, because God is the Creator of man. The Bible is the foremost diagnostic manual on humankind. Man's problems and diseases have already been assessed and diagnosed in God's Word. God's prescriptions have already been written for humankinds treatment, healing and restoration. God's Word has prescriptions for individuals, families, institutions and nations on how to be healed and how to be whole. It has directions and instructions on how to stay well and how to prevent illnesses. This concerted journey of truth and faith through God's Word will reveal answers, solutions, directions and resources in abundance for our troubled, pathological and crisis times. God promises not just abundant life, but eternal life through Jesus Christ as well.s

American Prayer
United States Declaration Of Repentance

Lord, we have violated the self- evidentiary truths that all men are created equal. We have violated the inalienable human rights of life, liberty and the pursuit of happiness of our brothers and sisters.

Our executive, legislative, judicial and corporate systems have denied equal rights and equal opportunities to certain citizens of the United States. We are guilty of enslaving and oppressing other selected human beings. We have denied truth, obstructed justice, violated goodness and practiced unrighteousness. We have rejected your undisputable sovereign authority. We have turned our backs on the outstretched arms of your love and grace.

Lord, our heads are confused; our hearts are hateful; our purposes are vain; our bodies are abused; our souls are lost. In lieu of growing up as enlightened men and women, we have chosen the naive prison house of childhood. You have created us as your children and given us your image; and yet, we seek other identities that are alien, idolatrous and contrary to your will. We have chosen sinful self-righteousness instead of your righteousness of truth.

Lord, forgive us for violating, selectively and arbitrarily, the laws of the U. S. Constitution and the Declaration of Independence. Forgive us for defaming your name on our currency, "In God We Trust." Forgive us for betraying the American Motto as, "One Nation Under God." Forgive us for ignoring the Biblical Word of Truth and for rejecting the Way, the Truth and the Life in Jesus Christ.

Lord, give us the spirit of repentance, atonement, restitution and restoration. Create in us, and in America, a clean heart and renew a right spirit within us.

In the name of the only Begotten Son and Savior, JESUS CHRIST. Amen

(Pastor W. J. Webb, U.S. Citizen)

Bibliography/References

The Holy Bible (King James Version)

American Psychiatric Association (1994), Diagnostic and Statistical Manual of Mental Disorders (4th ed.) Washington, DC: 1994.

American Psychiatric Association. Diagnostic and Statistical Manual of Mental Disorders (5th ed.) Washington, DC: 2013)

Appel, Willa. Cults in America-Programmed for Paradise. New York: Henry Holt and Company, 1983.

Buttrick, George Arthur (ed). The Interpreters Bible. New York: Abingdon Press, 1952.

Benne, Robert. The Paradoxical Vision, A Public Theology for the Twenty-first Century. Augsburg: Fortress Press, 1995.

Bright, John. A History of Israel. Philadelphia: Westminster Press, 1972.

Burns, James MacGregor. Government by the People. Englewood Cliffs: Prentice-Hall, 1963.

Blanchard, Ken and Hodges, Phil. The Servant Leader. Nashville: Thomas Nelson, 2003.

Carter, Stephen L. The Culture of Disbelief. New York: Random House, 1994.

Conkle, Daniel O. Constitutional Law, The Religious Clauses. New York: Foundation Press, 2003.

Cox, Harvey. The Secular City. New York: The MacMillan Company, 1995.

Dubois, W. F, B. The Souls of Black Folk. New York: Vintage Books, 1990.

Everly, George S. and Lating, Jeffrey. Psychotraumatology. New York: Plenum Press, 1995.

Egan. Gerard. The Skilled Helper. Boston: Brooks/Cole Publishing Co., 1998.

Fosdick, Harry Emerson. The Modern Use of the Bible. New York: McMillan Co., 1961.

Ford, David F. The Modern Theologians. Cambridge: Blackwell Publishers, 1989.

Harris, Stephen L. The New Testament, A Student's Introduction (4th ed), Boston: McGraw-Hill, 2002.

Mead, Frank S. Handbook of Denominations in the United States. Nashville: Abingdon Press, 1985.

Malkin, Michelle. Culture of Corruption. Washington, DC: Regnery Publishing, Inc., 2009.

Mason, Alpheus Thomas. American Constitutional Law, Introductory Essays and Selected Cases. Englewood Cliffs: Prentice-Hall, INC, 1978.

Montessori, Maria. The Absorbent Mind. New York: Dell Publishing, 1967.

Quarles, Benjamin. The Negro in the Making of America. New York: MacMillan Publishing Co., 1987.

Tillman, William M. Understanding Christian Ethics, An Interpretive Approach. Nashville: Broadman & Holman Publishers, 1988.

Strong, James. The New Strong Exhaustive Concordance. Nashville: Nelson Publishers, 1995.

The Constitution of the United State of America as Amended. U. S. Government Printing Office. Washington, DC, 2000.

Wallis, Jim. The Great Awakening, Reviving Faith & Politics in a Post Religious Right America. New York: HarperCollins Publishers, 2008.

Webb, Willie James. God's Spiritual Prescriptions, For Healing, Liberation and Salvation. Bloomington: AuthorHouse, 2001.

Webb, Willie James. The Way Out of Darkness, Vital Public Theology. Bloomington: AuthorHouse, 2007.

Webb, Willie James. Ezekiel Saw the Wheel, Can You See the Cross? Bloomington: AuthorHouse, 2014.

Webb, W. J. Hatred Addiction Recovery, Prescriptions for Wellness. USA: LitFire Publishing, 2018.

Printed in the United States
By Bookmasters